Blu

Written and Illustrated by Cindy M.

Copyright© Cindy Mackey, 2018

All rights reserved. This book or any portion thereof may not be reproduced or used in any manner whatsoever without the express written permission of the publisher.

Published in the United States of America by Cyrano Books
918 12th avenue suite 1000
Honolulu, HI 96816

ISBN: 978-1-7322739-0-0

www.cyranobooks.com

For Steve and Sue

Blu was once the brightest
fish in the sea.

But time passed ...

And his color began to fade away.

Everyone wanted to help Blu shine again.

The nurse fish nursed…

The cleaner fishes cleaned...

The eels brought him nutritious food to eat...

The angel fishes served him something to drink...

The lobsters turned on his favorite television show…

And the red snapper gave him a hat
to keep him warm.

But Puffer didn't know what he could do.

The End

www.ingramcontent.com/pod-product-compliance
Lightning Source LLC
Chambersburg PA
CBHW041116070526
44584CB00002B/189